Contents

WHAT IS THIS?
Faith Conversations for Mentors and Youth
by Franklin W. Nelson

Editors: Jeffrey S. Nelson and Virginia Bonde Zarth
Cover design: David Meyer
Cover photo copyright © 2001 PhotoDisc, Inc.
Interior illustration: Studio Arts

Scripture quotations are from New Revised Standard Version Bible, copyright © 1989 Division of Christian Education of the National Council of the Churches of Christ in the United States of America. Used by permission.

ISBN 0-8066-4254-8

Manufactured in U.S.A.

05   04   03   02   01   1   2   3   4   5   6   7   8   9   10

A Message to Mentors

Many faith communities have discovered that a positive and powerful dynamic is present when youth and adults get together for meaningful talks about the Christian faith. Welcome to this innovative way to help intergenerational communication happen in a natural and meaningful way for confirmation-age youth and adults. The tear-out conversations in this resource book can be used in one-on-one situations, but they also work well for small groups in which there is one mentor for more than one youth mentee. You'll notice that each tear-out conversation is duplicated; one copy is for the mentor and the other is for the mentee.

Martin Luther wrote the Small Catechism when his oldest child, Hans, was a toddler. He was influenced by the child's constant questioning, in German, *"Was ist das?"*—or in English, "What is this?" or "What does this mean for us?" It is a good question to ask throughout confirmation for both the mentor and mentee: "What is the meaning of the faith for us?" And so, we have taken the toddler's question to be the title for this resource.

The What Is This? series of resources was created for some of the same reasons Martin Luther wrote his Small Catechism. The talksheets in this book provide a guide for meaningful faith conversations, and make it more likely that "faith-full" conversations will take place between mentors and confirmation learners. Some mentors might say, "I don't really know how to talk about faith with a young person!" Let this resource be your guide. The process is simple, open-ended, and will help both you and your mentee become comfortable as you talk about life and faith together.

So, welcome, mentors! Welcome to the continuing adventure of faith. Welcome to some good times of sharing. Welcome to the joy of serving each other. Welcome to the satisfaction of knowing that you're making a positive difference in the life and faith of an adolescent confirmation learner. Welcome to the deepening of your own spiritual life and faith.

And thanks, mentors! Thanks for saying "Yes!" to being involved with a learner in What Is This? Thanks for your interest in the Christian faith and for being involved in your faith community. Thanks for being a person willing to grow in your faith and for being open to giving the gift of time and yourself. Thanks for being willing to take a risk.

This may be one of the best things you've ever done!

Confirmation—What Is This?

Confirmation is all about healthy relationships with God, others, and self!

Jesus said that the first and most important of all the commandments is to "love the Lord your God with all your heart, and with all your soul, and with all your mind, and with all your strength" (Mark 12:30). If we love God with heart, soul, mind, and strength, the health of our relationship with God increases. The same is true in our relationships with others, even the relationship we have with our own self. So Jesus continues, "You shall love your neighbor [others] as yourself" (Mark 12:31).

Many times in the Bible, human beings are compared to trees. The prophet Jeremiah said that those who trust in the Lord "shall be like a tree planted by water, sending out its roots by the stream" (Jeremiah 17:8). And Jesus said, "every good tree bears good fruit, but the bad tree bears bad fruit . . . you will know [people of faith] by their fruits" (Matthew 7:17, 20).

If our lives are to be fruitful, we need to put down healthy roots in the soil of love. That means that our relationships with God, others, and self need to be full of love. That's why healthy, life-giving families and faith communities are essential to the well-being of children and youth. Love gives young people the roots they need to live fruitful lives.

Baptism is the beginning of this rooting in grace, love, and faith. Adolescent *confirmation* is an important affirmation of this baptismal journey of faith.

To be *confirmed* means, literally, to be "with firmness." A tree that is "confirmed" has its roots planted firmly in life-giving soil. A person who is confirmed is one who is developing a healthy root system in the soil of loving relationships with God, others, and self, nourished by the water of Baptism. To be confirmed in faith, therefore, is to have our lives firmly planted in the love of God, others, and self.

How to Use What Is This?

The conversation starters in this resource offer an easy way to create an environment of good communication between youth and their mentors.

If you haven't had a chance to review one of the talksheets in this resource book, turn to one now to see how each conversation is organized. You'll notice that it is like a conversational map to follow. Each person has a talksheet. The conversation begins with introductory words followed by a section of sentence completions. Because of the open-ended nature of the sentence completions, each person can be as personal and honest as he or she wants. The content of the conversation is entirely up to those who are involved.

Note that each conversation talksheet is duplicated—one page is for the mentor and the other is for the youth. This process recognizes that good communication requires more than being a good talker. What Is This? invites each person in the conversation to think silently about what they want to say before they say it.

The reading and writing step is very important! Some may feel inadequate in their spelling and writing ability. Be reassured, and reassure your mentee, that the talksheets are not turned in or seen by anyone else. Write what first comes to mind, and if nothing does, leave the space blank and move on. The important thing is not what is written, but what is talked about. The writing step serves only to provide equal time for both of you to think about what you will want to say when you begin talking.

Good communication is mutual, that is, each person needs to feel that they have a chance to speak about what they want to say. What Is This? conversation starters equalize the conversation and help both mentor and mentee to be "on the same page" with each other. This is especially important with adult/youth conversations in order to create an atmosphere of mutual communication.

Two Options

1. What Is This? may be used one-on-one away from the group setting, in a restaurant, on a park bench, or in a home setting.

2. What Is This? may be used in group settings in your congregation or on confirmation retreats. It is important that you take time to read the next pages of background material about the mentor's role in passing on the faith, and also, how this communication process works. It is especially important that you take the time to experience the first conversation designed specifically for mentor training, "Preparing to Be a Mentor." Many churches will want to use this talksheet as part of an evening of orientation for mentors. Follow the step-by-step instructions:

Step One: Tear out the duplicate sheets.
Step Two: Set aside an hour for the conversation.
Step Three: Follow the step-by-step process.

Choose, Help, Esteem, Know (CHEK)

Your primary role as a mentor is to lead the way in CHOOSING, HELPING, ESTEEMING, and KNOWING the youth God has placed in your guidance and care. Remember that it is God's Spirit of love that produces the wisdom you will need for this relationship.

Pray. Rely on God's guidance and wisdom. Pray daily for your mentee, and pray before those times when you have What Is This? conversations. Remember that God has a way of supporting and guiding us in the primary relationships of our lives. Trust in God and, like a tree planted by water, let your life be fruitful.

A CHEK-list for healthy mentor/mentee relationships:

Your role is to Choose (say yes to) your mentee.

- Commit yourself to having regular talks with your mentee.
- Be interested in him or her.
- Pray for your mentee often.
- Invite informal conversation about his or her activities and interests.
- Follow up on conversations you've already had, for example, "How did it go last Friday?"
- Can you think of others?

Your role is to Help (serve) your mentee.

- Be available, but not pushy.
- Avoid evaluating your mentee's ideas or life. Instead, listen attentively.
- Be patient! God isn't finished with any of us yet.
- Make a commitment to help your mentee with transportation and funding for confirmation activities/retreats.
- Offer to tell stories from your own life, but avoid sounding like an authority. None of us has all the answers. Be willing to share your own questions and doubts.
- Be ready to explore options and offer suggestions and ideas that will guide your mentee in his/her thinking and deciding; but encourage your mentee to make her/his own choices and decisions.
- Present the Christian life in a positive light. Help your mentee to see the value of living life as a follower of Jesus Christ by living your life as a follower of Christ.
- Model involvement in the church by being involved yourself.
- Model the importance of prayer and scripture reading by praying and reading the Bible.
- Can you think of others?

Your role is to Esteem (accept) your mentee.

- Accept your mentee unconditionally. Look past all that may seem unlovable to you and try to notice all that is lovable.
- Respect your mentee as an individual who has the right to make her/his own choices. Your primary role is to enjoy and love your mentee rather than to judge or control him/her.

- Affirm. Don't just think a compliment, say it.
- Write a note or letter expressing how proud you are of your mentee.
- Adjust your schedule to make time for him or her.
- Remember to make a note of details your mentee mentions to you.
- E-mail, telephone, or send a note. Stay in touch regularly.
- Can you think of others?

Your role is to Know your mentee.

- Listen carefully. Resist doing all the talking. Give your mentee time and space.
- Be patient.
- Be honest. Let your mentee know who you are. Model being honest and open, and it will help your mentee to be more willing to let you know her/him.
- Learn what your mentee is interested in. Notice his or her qualities and skills, and invite her or him to talk about life goals and desires.
- Be interested in what interests your mentee. Listen to his or her music. Watch TV together. Go to a movie and talk about it afterwards.
- Can you think of others?

Your role is not to have the answers.

You may feel inadequate in your knowledge of the Bible and the Christian faith. If you are like most people, you have questions and doubts of your own. Healthy Christian relationships don't usually happen because one person in the relationship knows all the correct answers and feeds them to the other person. Healthy mentor/mentee relationships depend on our openness, realizing that we each have much to learn as we try to live out our baptismal faith and follow Jesus Christ as one of his disciples. (The word *disciple* means "student" or "learner.")

Thanks once again for saying "Yes!" to being a mentor and taking the time to grow a healthier relationship with a young person in confirmation.

Preparing to Be a Mentor

Mentor: A wise and trusted friend and guide.

1. Introduction

Thanks for your willingness to be an adult friend and guide with a confirmation-age youth. Mentoring is one of the most effective ways you can make a positive difference in the life and faith of a young person.

2. Three Options

Three options for using this talksheet:

1. Use in small mentor groups as part of a mentor training and orientation event.

2. Meet with one other mentor to write and talk.

3. Reflect, write, and pray on your own as you think about your role as a mentor.

3. Journal Notes

Use a pen or pencil to write a response for each of the following:

When I Was in My Early Teens

1. I enjoyed (doing what?) . . .

2. I also spent a lot of time . . .

3. One of my best friends was _____ and we used to . . .

4. A person who valued and accepted me was _____, by the way she/he . . .

5. I sometimes wondered if . . .

6. One of my best days was the time . . .

7. One of my worst days was the time . . .

8. This is how I'd describe the relationship I had with my parent(s) or guardian(s) . . .

9. School, for me, was . . .

10. To me, the church was a place where . . .

4. Talk and Listen

When you both have finished writing, take turns talking about each of your responses. If you have time, continue with Side 2. If not, come back to Side 2 in the near future.

Preparing to Be a Mentor

1. Scripture Talk

Each of the tear-out mentor/youth conversations in this book invites you to read and discuss a scripture passage.

And this is his commandment, that we should believe in the name of his Son Jesus Christ and love one another, just as he has commanded us. All who obey his commandments abide in him, and he abides in them. And by this we know that he abides in us, by the Spirit that he has given us. 1 John 3:23-24

Discuss

1. This scripture passage suggests that if I am to be an effective mentor, I will need to . . .

2. For me to believe in the name of Jesus Christ means that I . . .

3. For me to love a young person in the way Christ would love him or her means that I . . .

2. Journal Notes

Use a pen or pencil to write a response for each of the following:

The Role of a Mentor

1. I chose to be a mentor with youth because . . .

2. Some of the feelings or questions I have about being a mentor include . . .

3. More than anything young people today need (make a list) . . .

4. Parents and adults need to try to understand that youth . . .

5. It's important for the faith community to take an active role in helping young people grow in their Christian faith because . . .

6. Some of the ways that I, as a mentor, can show I care for the youth I'll be mentoring include (make a list) . . .

7. As a mentor I am willing to . . .

8. Looking back on the experience a year from now I want to able to say that I was able to help the youth to . . .

and the confirmation-age youth helped me to . . .

9. My prayer: Dear God, help the young person(s) I am planning to mentor . . .

and help me to . . .

3. Talk and Listen

When you both have finished writing, take turns talking about each of your responses.

Preparing to Be a Mentor

Mentor: A wise and trusted friend and guide.

1. Introduction

Thanks for your willingness to be an adult friend and guide with a confirmation-age youth. Mentoring is one of the most effective ways you can make a positive difference in the life and faith of a young person.

2. Three Options

Three options for using this talksheet:

1. Use in small mentor groups as part of a mentor training and orientation event.

2. Meet with one other mentor to write and talk.

3. Reflect, write, and pray on your own as you think about your role as a mentor.

3. Journal Notes

Use a pen or pencil to write a response for each of the following:

When I Was in My Early Teens

1. I enjoyed (doing what?) . . .

2. I also spent a lot of time . . .

3. One of my best friends was _____ and we used to . . .

4. A person who valued and accepted me was _____, by the way she/he . . .

5. I sometimes wondered if . . .

6. One of my best days was the time . . .

7. One of my worst days was the time . . .

8. This is how I'd describe the relationship I had with my parent(s) or guardian(s) . . .

9. School, for me, was . . .

10. To me, the church was a place where . . .

4. Talk and Listen

When you both have finished writing, take turns talking about each of your responses. If you have time, continue with Side 2. If not, come back to Side 2 in the near future.

Preparing to Be a Mentor

1. Scripture Talk
Each of the tear-out mentor/youth conversations in this book invites you to read and discuss a scripture passage.

And this is his commandment, that we should believe in the name of his Son Jesus Christ and love one another, just as he has commanded us. All who obey his commandments abide in him, and he abides in them. And by this we know that he abides in us, by the Spirit that he has given us. 1 John 3:23-24

Discuss
1. This scripture passage suggests that if I am to be an effective mentor, I will need to . . .

2. For me to believe in the name of Jesus Christ means that I . . .

3. For me to love a young person in the way Christ would love him or her means that I . . .

2. Journal Notes
Use a pen or pencil to write a response for each of the following:

The Role of a Mentor
1. I chose to be a mentor with youth because . . .

2. Some of the feelings or questions I have about being a mentor include . . .

3. More than anything young people today need (make a list) . . .

4. Parents and adults need to try to understand that youth . . .

5. It's important for the faith community to take an active role in helping young people grow in their Christian faith because . . .

6. Some of the ways that I, as a mentor, can show I care for the youth I'll be mentoring include (make a list) . . .

7. As a mentor I am willing to . . .

8. Looking back on the experience a year from now I want to able to say that I was able to help the youth to . . .

and the confirmation-age youth helped me to . . .

9. My prayer: Dear God, help the young person(s) I am planning to mentor . . .

and help me to . . .

3. Talk and Listen
When you both have finished writing, take turns talking about each of your responses.

Why Be Confirmed?

1. Introduction

Welcome to the confirmation journey. You have been traveling the road of life and faith for quite a while since you were baptized. There has been much along the way to enjoy and learn. Jesus invites all who want to be his disciples to follow him and to walk with him in the journey of life and faith. May God strengthen you on the way!

2. Scripture Talk

In all your ways acknowledge [God], and he will make straight your paths. Proverbs 3:6

Discuss

1. "In all your ways" means . . .

2. As I think of my life's journey, some of the ways God may want to direct and lead me include . . .

3. To "acknowledge" God means that I . . .

3. Journal Notes

Use a pen or pencil to write a response for each of the following:

Let Me Tell You a Little about Myself

1. My full name is

_____.

2. Six words that describe me are . . .

3. As a young child one of my favorite places to go was . . .

4. Some childhood games I liked to play were . . .

Things I Like

5. My favorite ice cream is . . .

6. When I order a pizza, I like to order . . .

7. A song or kind of music I like to listen to is . . .

8. I like to shop (where?) . . .

9. I like it when people . . .

10. One person I like being around is _____, because . . .

11. Some things about our church that I like include . . .

12. Something about myself I like is . . .

13. Something I like about being the age I am is . . .

14. One of the best days of my life was the day that . . .

4. Talk and Listen

When you both have finished writing, take turns talking about each of your responses. If you have time, continue with Side 2. If not, come back to Side 2 in the near future.

Why Be Confirmed?

1. What Is This?

When Martin Luther wrote the Small Catechism, "What is this?" was the question he often asked. During each of your talks you will be invited to discuss some of Luther's writing in a section called "What Is This?" The First Article of the Apostles' Creed is this: "I believe in God, the Father almighty, creator of heaven and earth." Luther asks, "What is this?" Here's part of his answer: "I believe that God has created me together with all creatures . . . For all of this I owe it to God to thank and praise, serve and obey him. This is most certainly true."

Discuss

1. This is what I believe about the creation of the world:

2. One question I have about creation is . . .

3. Do you agree that we "owe it to God" to live our lives for God? Why or why not?

2. Journal Notes

Use a pen or pencil to write a response for each of the following:

1. If I could travel anywhere in the world, I'd like to travel to . . .

And I'd like to invite _____ to go with me because he or she . . .

2. Life is like a long journey with many challenges along the way. Some of the challenges or difficulties I have had to face so far in life include . . .

3. Confirmation is a lot like a journey, too. If someone asked me, "Why do you think confirmation is important?" I'd say . . .

4. The word *confirm* means to establish "with firmness" the truth or accuracy of something. To be confirmed in the Christian faith means that I am coming to believe firmly that . . .

5. I think I can get the most out of my confirmation journey if I am willing to . . .

6. In our mentor/youth relationship, I'm looking forward to . . .

7. Here's a confirmation prayer for you/me/us as we begin this journey: Dear God, . . .

3. Talk and Listen

When you both have finished writing, take turns talking about each of your responses.

4. Scripture Talk

Discuss Philippians 4:1: **Stand firm in the Lord.**

5. If You Have Time, Talk About . . .

1. One of the best trips or vacations I ever took was . . .

2. My worst adventure was . . .

3. My "dream vacation" was . . .

4. How I pack a suitcase for a trip . . .

Why Be Confirmed?

1. Introduction

Welcome to the confirmation journey. You have been traveling the road of life and faith for quite a while since you were baptized. There has been much along the way to enjoy and learn. Jesus invites all who want to be his disciples to follow him and to walk with him in the journey of life and faith. May God strengthen you on the way!

2. Scripture Talk

In all your ways acknowledge [God], and he will make straight your paths. Proverbs 3:6

Discuss

1. "In all your ways" means . . .

2. As I think of my life's journey, some of the ways God may want to direct and lead me include . . .

3. To "acknowledge" God means that I . . .

3. Journal Notes

Use a pen or pencil to write a response for each of the following:

Let Me Tell You a Little about Myself

1. My full name is

_____.

2. Six words that describe me are . . .

3. As a young child one of my favorite places to go was . . .

4. Some childhood games I liked to play were . . .

Things I Like

5. My favorite ice cream is . . .

6. When I order a pizza, I like to order . . .

7. A song or kind of music I like to listen to is . . .

8. I like to shop (where?) . . .

9. I like it when people . . .

10. One person I like being around is _____, because . . .

11. Some things about our church that I like include . . .

12. Something about myself I like is . . .

13. Something I like about being the age I am is . . .

14. One of the best days of my life was the day that . . .

4. Talk and Listen

When you both have finished writing, take turns talking about each of your responses. If you have time, continue with Side 2. If not, come back to Side 2 in the near future.

Why Be Confirmed?

1. What Is This?
When Martin Luther wrote the Small Catechism, "What is this?" was the question he often asked. During each of your talks you will be invited to discuss some of Luther's writing in a section called "What Is This?" The First Article of the Apostles' Creed is this: "I believe in God, the Father almighty, creator of heaven and earth." Luther asks, "What is this?" Here's part of his answer: "I believe that God has created me together with all creatures . . . For all of this I owe it to God to thank and praise, serve and obey him. This is most certainly true."

Discuss
1. This is what I believe about the creation of the world:

2. One question I have about creation is . . .

3. Do you agree that we "owe it to God" to live our lives for God? Why or why not?

2. Journal Notes
Use a pen or pencil to write a response for each of the following:

1. If I could travel anywhere in the world, I'd like to travel to . . .

And I'd like to invite _____ to go with me because he or she . . .

2. Life is like a long journey with many challenges along the way. Some of the challenges or difficulties I have had to face so far in life include . . .

3. Confirmation is a lot like a journey, too. If someone asked me, "Why do you think confirmation is important?" I'd say . . .

4. The word *confirm* means to establish "with firmness" the truth or accuracy of something. To be confirmed in the Christian faith means that I am coming to believe firmly that . . .

5. I think I can get the most out of my confirmation journey if I am willing to . . .

6. In our mentor/youth relationship, I'm looking forward to . . .

7. Here's a confirmation prayer for you/me/us as we begin this journey: Dear God, . . .

3. Talk and Listen
When you both have finished writing, take turns talking about each of your responses.

4. Scripture Talk
Discuss Philippians 4:1: **Stand firm in the Lord.**

5. If You Have Time, Talk About . . .
1. One of the best trips or vacations I ever took was . . .

2. My worst adventure was . . .

3. My "dream vacation" was . . .

4. How I pack a suitcase for a trip . . .

Following Jesus

1. Introduction

When you plan a trip, lots of decisions need to be made: Where do I want to go? Who will go with me? How much will the trip cost? The journey of life and faith involves making a lot of choices, too. When Jesus invites us to follow him, he invites us to let him walk with us as our guide throughout life. May you discover the love and joy that are possible when you choose to travel Christ's way. Have a great trip!

2. Journal Notes

Use a pen or pencil to write a response for each of the following:

1. When I was a little child, a person I looked up to and wanted to be like was _____ because he/she . . .

2. More recently, a person who has had a positive influence on my life is _____. Explain how:

3. I am more likely to respect and follow a person who has the following qualities of leadership:

Circle the number that shows to what extent you agree with the following statements:

4. Jesus is the unique Son of God.

I doubt   I agree
it   1 2 3 4 5 6 7 totally

Explain what you think it means to say that Jesus is the Son of God.

5. Jesus is the Lord and Leader of my life.

Not   Yes,
really 1 2 3 4 5 6 7 totally

Explain what you think it means to call Jesus the Lord/Leader of your life.

6. After dying on the cross, Jesus came back to life and continues to be alive in the world today.

I doubt   I agree
it   1 2 3 4 5 6 7 totally

Explain what you believe about the resurrection of Jesus.

7. Jesus is the one who, more than anyone, helps us to know God.

I doubt   I agree
it   1 2 3 4 5 6 7 totally

What can we learn from Jesus about the nature of God?

3. Talk and Listen

When you both have finished writing, take turns talking about each of your responses.

4. Scripture Talk

[Jesus said], "If any want to become my followers, let them deny themselves and take up their cross and follow me. For those who want to save their life will lose it, and those who lose their life for my sake, and for the sake of the gospel, will save it." Mark 8:34-35

Discuss

1. When Jesus says that I need to "lose" my life, I think he means that I need to . . .

2. It might be easier for me to follow Jesus if I were sure that . . .

5. Continue on Side 2

If you have time, continue with Side 2. If not, come back to Side 2 in the near future.

Following Jesus

1. What Is This?

Martin Luther asks: "What then is the significance of such a baptism with water? It signifies that the old person in us with all sins and evil desires is to be drowned daily through sorrow for sin and repentance, and that daily a new person is to come forth and rise up to live before God in righteousness and purity forever."

Discuss

1. The date of my own baptism was . . .

2. I think that Baptism is important, because it shows that even though we sin and have evil desires, God still . . .

3. To say that I am living my Christian faith means that I . . .

2. Journal Notes

Use a pen or pencil to write a response for each of the following:

1. When Jesus invited his disciples to follow him, I think he was asking them to . . .

2. Through the centuries men and women have been willing to follow Jesus (even to their death) because they believed . . .

3. To promise that I will follow Jesus means that I am willing to . . .

4. To say that I have chosen to be a disciple of Jesus means that . . .

5. Jesus loved others by giving his life. If I am to love others as Jesus did, it means that in my relationships I will need to . . .

6. Jesus always did what was right and invited his followers to do the right thing, too. In my life, lately, one thing I could change in order to do the right thing is . . .

7. My prayer as a follower of Jesus is: Dear God, help me to . . .

3. Talk and Listen

When you both have finished writing, take turns talking about each of your responses.

4. Scripture Talk

Discuss John 13:34: **[Jesus said], "Just as I have loved you, you also should love one another."**

5. If You Have Time . . .

Play the game "mirror." Standing works best. One person acts as a mirror while the other person stands in front of the "mirror" making movements and gestures. The one who is the mirror has to match the movements of the other. Switch roles, then talk about how this is an illustration of what it means to follow Jesus.

Following Jesus

1. Introduction

When you plan a trip, lots of decisions need to be made: Where do I want to go? Who will go with me? How much will the trip cost? The journey of life and faith involves making a lot of choices, too. When Jesus invites us to follow him, he invites us to let him walk with us as our guide throughout life. May you discover the love and joy that are possible when you choose to travel Christ's way. Have a great trip!

2. Journal Notes

Use a pen or pencil to write a response for each of the following:

1. When I was a little child, a person I looked up to and wanted to be like was _____ because he/she . . .

2. More recently, a person who has had a positive influence on my life is _____. Explain how:

3. I am more likely to respect and follow a person who has the following qualities of leadership:

Circle the number that shows to what extent you agree with the following statements:

4. Jesus is the unique Son of God.

I doubt it   1   2   3   4   5   6   7   I agree totally

Explain what you think it means to say that Jesus is the Son of God.

5. Jesus is the Lord and Leader of my life.

Not really   1   2   3   4   5   6   7   Yes, totally

Explain what you think it means to call Jesus the Lord/Leader of your life.

6. After dying on the cross, Jesus came back to life and continues to be alive in the world today.

I doubt it   1   2   3   4   5   6   7   I agree totally

Explain what you believe about the resurrection of Jesus.

7. Jesus is the one who, more than anyone, helps us to know God.

I doubt it   1   2   3   4   5   6   7   I agree totally

What can we learn from Jesus about the nature of God?

3. Talk and Listen

When you both have finished writing, take turns talking about each of your responses.

4. Scripture Talk

[Jesus said], "If any want to become my followers, let them deny themselves and take up their cross and follow me. For those who want to save their life will lose it, and those who lose their life for my sake, and for the sake of the gospel, will save it." Mark 8:34-35

Discuss

1. When Jesus says that I need to "lose" my life, I think he means that I need to . . .

2. It might be easier for me to follow Jesus if I were sure that . . .

5. Continue on Side 2

If you have time, continue with Side 2. If not, come back to Side 2 in the near future.

Following Jesus

1. What Is This?

Martin Luther asks: "What then is the significance of such a baptism with water? It signifies that the old person in us with all sins and evil desires is to be drowned daily through sorrow for sin and repentance, and that daily a new person is to come forth and rise up to live before God in righteousness and purity forever."

Discuss

1. The date of my own baptism was . . .

2. I think that Baptism is important, because it shows that even though we sin and have evil desires, God still . . .

3. To say that I am living my Christian faith means that I . . .

2. Journal Notes

Use a pen or pencil to write a response for each of the following:

1. When Jesus invited his disciples to follow him, I think he was asking them to . . .

2. Through the centuries men and women have been willing to follow Jesus (even to their death) because they believed . . .

3. To promise that I will follow Jesus means that I am willing to . . .

4. To say that I have chosen to be a disciple of Jesus means that . . .

5. Jesus loved others by giving his life. If I am to love others as Jesus did, it means that in my relationships I will need to . . .

6. Jesus always did what was right and invited his followers to do the right thing, too. In my life, lately, one thing I could change in order to do the right thing is . . .

7. My prayer as a follower of Jesus is: Dear God, help me to . . .

3. Talk and Listen

When you both have finished writing, take turns talking about each of your responses.

4. Scripture Talk

Discuss John 13:34: **[Jesus said], "Just as I have loved you, you also should love one another."**

5. If You Have Time . . .

Play the game "mirror." Standing works best. One person acts as a mirror while the other person stands in front of the "mirror" making movements and gestures. The one who is the mirror has to match the movements of the other. Switch roles, then talk about how this is an illustration of what it means to follow Jesus.

Why the Church?

1. Introduction

If you have ever taken a trip with someone, you know that traveling with others can help make it more enjoyable and interesting—and sometimes more challenging. When we live the Christian life, we join others who are traveling the Christian way with us. The church is a worldwide faith community of all those who are following Jesus as the Lord of their life. May you know the joy and strength that comes from belonging to the church.

2. Journal Notes

Use a pen or pencil to write a response for each of the following:

1. Something I have enjoyed recently in my faith community is . . .

2. Three reasons I am a part of my faith community include:
-
-
-

3. If a friend asked me, "What difference does being a part of a faith community make in your life?" I might say . . .

4. A person in my faith community who has helped me feel welcome is _____. She/he made me feel welcome by . . .

5. Some of the questions I have about the church are . . .

6. Three wishes or hopes I have for my faith community include . . .
-
-
-

7. Here's my own definition for the word *church:* The church is . . .

8. If I couldn't be a part of my faith community, I would especially miss . . .

3. Talk and Listen

When you both have finished writing, take turns talking about each of your responses.

4. Scripture Talk

[Jesus said], **"For where two or three are gathered in my name, I am there among them."** Matthew 18:20

Discuss

1. When I get together with others to learn about Jesus Christ and worship God, I think it really helps me to . . .

2. Having these mentor/youth talks is helping me to . . .

5. Continue on Side 2

If you have time, continue with Side 2. If not, come back to Side 2 in the near future.

Why the Church?

1. What Is This?

The Third Article of the Apostles' Creed says, "I believe in the Holy Spirit, the holy catholic Church, the communion of saints . . ." What is this? Luther explains: "I believe that by my own understanding or strength I cannot believe in Jesus Christ my Lord or come to him, but instead the Holy Spirit has called me through the gospel, enlightened me with his gifts, made me holy, and kept me in the true faith, just as he calls, gathers, enlightens, and makes holy the whole Christian church on earth and keeps it with Jesus Christ in the one common, true faith."

Discuss

1. The word *catholic* means "universal." What is universal about the church?

2. I think the "communion of saints" refers to . . .

3. I would describe the "one common, true faith" as . . .

2. Journal Notes

Use a pen or pencil to write a response for each of the following:

1. If Jesus came in person to speak to our faith community this coming Sunday and told us his reasons for calling together the church, I think he might say, "I called the church together so that . . ."

2. Jesus might add, "A faith community is a healthy community if the members . . ."

3. Three things my faith community is doing that fulfill what Jesus wants the church to be doing are . . .
-
-
-

4. Three things my faith community needs to start doing or do better are . . .
-
-
-

5. If I said to someone, "I am really involved in my faith community," it would mean that I . . .

6. And if he or she asked, "Why do you think it's important to attend church regularly?" I would say . . .

7. Some ways I could (or would like to be) more involved in my faith community include . . .

8. For my faith community I pray: Dear God, . . .

3. Talk and Listen

When you both have finished writing, take turns talking about each of your responses.

4. Scripture Talk

Discuss 1 Corinthians 12:27: **Now you are the body of Christ and individually members of it.**

5. If You Have Time, Talk About . . .

1. Worship experiences. What helps you feel close to God? What songs lead you to experience worship? What is worship?

2. Youth involvement. How are the youth of your faith community involved in the life of the whole church? Could the youth be more involved than they are? How?

Why the Church?

1. Introduction

If you have ever taken a trip with someone, you know that traveling with others can help make it more enjoyable and interesting—and sometimes more challenging. When we live the Christian life, we join others who are traveling the Christian way with us. The church is a worldwide faith community of all those who are following Jesus as the Lord of their life. May you know the joy and strength that comes from belonging to the church.

2. Journal Notes

Use a pen or pencil to write a response for each of the following:

1. Something I have enjoyed recently in my faith community is . . .

2. Three reasons I am a part of my faith community include:
-
-
-

3. If a friend asked me, "What difference does being a part of a faith community make in your life?" I might say . . .

4. A person in my faith community who has helped me feel welcome is _____. She/he made me feel welcome by . . .

5. Some of the questions I have about the church are . . .

6. Three wishes or hopes I have for my faith community include . . .
-
-
-

7. Here's my own definition for the word *church:* The church is . . .

8. If I couldn't be a part of my faith community, I would especially miss . . .

3. Talk and Listen

When you both have finished writing, take turns talking about each of your responses.

4. Scripture Talk

[Jesus said], "For where two or three are gathered in my name, I am there among them." Matthew 18:20

Discuss

1. When I get together with others to learn about Jesus Christ and worship God, I think it really helps me to . . .

2. Having these mentor/youth talks is helping me to . . .

5. Continue on Side 2

If you have time, continue with Side 2. If not, come back to Side 2 in the near future.

Why the Church?

1. What Is This?

The Third Article of the Apostles' Creed says, "I believe in the Holy Spirit, the holy catholic Church, the communion of saints . . ." What is this? Luther explains: "I believe that by my own understanding or strength I cannot believe in Jesus Christ my Lord or come to him, but instead the Holy Spirit has called me through the gospel, enlightened me with his gifts, made me holy, and kept me in the true faith, just as he calls, gathers, enlightens, and makes holy the whole Christian church on earth and keeps it with Jesus Christ in the one common, true faith."

Discuss

1. The word *catholic* means "universal." What is universal about the church?

2. I think the "communion of saints" refers to . . .

3. I would describe the "one common, true faith" as . . .

2. Journal Notes

Use a pen or pencil to write a response for each of the following:

1. If Jesus came in person to speak to our faith community this coming Sunday and told us his reasons for calling together the church, I think he might say, "I called the church together so that . . ."

2. Jesus might add, "A faith community is a healthy community if the members . . ."

3. Three things my faith community is doing that fulfill what Jesus wants the church to be doing are . . .
-
-
-

4. Three things my faith community needs to start doing or do better are . . .
-
-
-

5. If I said to someone, "I am really involved in my faith community," it would mean that I . . .

6. And if he or she asked, "Why do you think it's important to attend church regularly?" I would say . . .

7. Some ways I could (or would like to be) more involved in my faith community include . . .

8. For my faith community I pray: Dear God, . . .

3. Talk and Listen

When you both have finished writing, take turns talking about each of your responses.

4. Scripture Talk

Discuss 1 Corinthians 12:27: **Now you are the body of Christ and individually members of it.**

5. If You Have Time, Talk About . . .

1. Worship experiences. What helps you feel close to God? What songs lead you to experience worship? What is worship?

2. Youth involvement. How are the youth of your faith community involved in the life of the whole church? Could the youth be more involved than they are? How?

My Mission

1. Introduction

Choosing a direction, purpose, or mission in life can be hard. But once you've chosen where you want to go, it's much easier to figure out how you're going to get there, because now you can set your priorities and decide what's most important. What is your purpose in life? What do you aim to become? Remembering our baptism daily invites us to ask the question, "What do I want to do with my life today?" And when Jesus invites us to follow him, he also wants us to ask, "What does God want me to do with the rest of my life?" May God guide you in discovering your mission as you live the baptismal journey of faith.

2. Journal Notes

Use a pen or pencil to write a response for each of the following:

1. Three things I own that are important to me include . . .
-
-
-

2. Three people who are important to me are . . .
-
-
-

3. Three beliefs or values that are important to me include . . .
-
-
-

4. If someone asked me, "What's the most important thing in your life right now?" I would say . . .

5. From what I know about Jesus Christ, the most important thing in his life (the thing he taught, lived, and died for—his mission) was to . . .

6. If I said that I am committed to living the cause and mission of Jesus Christ, it would mean that I am willing to . . .

7. Some questions I have about my future and my mission and purpose in life are . . .

3. Talk and Listen

When you both have finished writing, take turns talking about each of your responses.

4. Scripture Talk

[Jesus said], "I came that [you] may have life, and have it abundantly." John 10:10

Discuss

1. Jesus is saying that his mission in life is to help people to . . .

2. I would describe my life as "abundant" when . . .

5. Continue on Side 2

If you have time, continue with Side 2. If not, come back to Side 2 in the near future.

My Mission

1. What Is This?

Martin Luther quotes the Lord's Prayer, "Your will be done, on earth as in heaven," and then asks: "What is this?" His answer? "God's good and gracious will comes about without our prayer, but we ask in this prayer that it may also come about in and among us . . . And God's will is done whenever God strengthens us and keeps us steadfast in his Word and in faith until the end of our lives."

Discuss

1. To want God's will to be done on earth as in heaven means that we are willing to . . .

2. Try to give an example of how God's good and gracious will can come about in us and among us.

2. Journal Notes

Use a pen or pencil to write a response for each of the following:

1. A clear mission and purpose can help us define our priorities. Three of my top priorities right now in my life include . . .

-
-
-

2. A clear mission can give us the inner strength and security to meet the difficult challenges of life. A challenge I am facing right now in my own life that I could use God's help and strength with is . . .

3. A clear mission can motivate us and give us energy and a willingness to work with persistence toward a goal. I would like to be more motivated in reaching the following goals:

-
-
-

4. If a person's mission is their main purpose for living, the direction they want to go in their life, and the thing they want to achieve more than anything else, then I would say that my overall mission or purpose in my life is to . . . (Describe in detail.)

5. My prayer as I try to live this mission is: Dear God, help me to . . .

3. Talk and Listen

When you both have finished writing, take turns talking about each of your responses.

4. Scripture Talk

Discuss Matthew 28:19-20: **[Jesus said], "Go therefore and make disciples of all nations, baptizing them . . . and teaching them to obey everything that I have commanded you."**

5. If You Have Time, Talk About . . .

1. The goal or mission of an athlete is to . . .

2. The goal or mission of a teacher is to . . .

3. The goal or mission of a student is to . . .

4. What difference has it made in your life when you have had a goal or a clear mission or direction in mind?

My Mission

1. Introduction

Choosing a direction, purpose, or mission in life can be hard. But once you've chosen where you want to go, it's much easier to figure out how you're going to get there, because now you can set your priorities and decide what's most important. What is your purpose in life? What do you aim to become? Remembering our baptism daily invites us to ask the question, "What do I want to do with my life today?" And when Jesus invites us to follow him, he also wants us to ask, "What does God want me to do with the rest of my life?" May God guide you in discovering your mission as you live the baptismal journey of faith.

2. Journal Notes

Use a pen or pencil to write a response for each of the following:

1. Three things I own that are important to me include . . .
-
-
-

2. Three people who are important to me are . . .
-
-
-

3. Three beliefs or values that are important to me include . . .
-
-
-

4. If someone asked me, "What's the most important thing in your life right now?" I would say . . .

5. From what I know about Jesus Christ, the most important thing in his life (the thing he taught, lived, and died for—his mission) was to . . .

6. If I said that I am committed to living the cause and mission of Jesus Christ, it would mean that I am willing to . . .

7. Some questions I have about my future and my mission and purpose in life are . . .

3. Talk and Listen

When you both have finished writing, take turns talking about each of your responses.

4. Scripture Talk

[Jesus said], "I came that [you] may have life, and have it abundantly." John 10:10

Discuss

1. Jesus is saying that his mission in life is to help people to . . .

2. I would describe my life as "abundant" when . . .

5. Continue on Side 2

If you have time, continue with Side 2. If not, come back to Side 2 in the near future.

My Mission

1. What Is This?

Martin Luther quotes the Lord's Prayer, "Your will be done, on earth as in heaven," and then asks: "What is this?" His answer? "God's good and gracious will comes about without our prayer, but we ask in this prayer that it may also come about in and among us . . . And God's will is done whenever God strengthens us and keeps us steadfast in his Word and in faith until the end of our lives."

Discuss

1. To want God's will to be done on earth as in heaven means that we are willing to . . .

2. Try to give an example of how God's good and gracious will can come about in us and among us.

2. Journal Notes

Use a pen or pencil to write a response for each of the following:

1. A clear mission and purpose can help us define our priorities. Three of my top priorities right now in my life include . . .

  •

  •

  •

2. A clear mission can give us the inner strength and security to meet the difficult challenges of life. A challenge I am facing right now in my own life that I could use God's help and strength with is . . .

3. A clear mission can motivate us and give us energy and a willingness to work with persistence toward a goal. I would like to be more motivated in reaching the following goals:

  •

  •

  •

4. If a person's mission is their main purpose for living, the direction they want to go in their life, and the thing they want to achieve more than anything else, then I would say that my overall mission or purpose in my life is to . . . (Describe in detail.)

5. My prayer as I try to live this mission is: Dear God, help me to . . .

3. Talk and Listen

When you both have finished writing, take turns talking about each of your responses.

4. Scripture Talk

Discuss Matthew 28:19-20: **[Jesus said], "Go therefore and make disciples of all nations, baptizing them . . . and teaching them to obey everything that I have commanded you."**

5. If You Have Time, Talk About . . .

1. The goal or mission of an athlete is to . . .

2. The goal or mission of a teacher is to . . .

3. The goal or mission of a student is to . . .

4. What difference has it made in your life when you have had a goal or a clear mission or direction in mind?

Living in the Spirit

1. Introduction

Genesis 1:2 describes the Spirit of the Creator God as moving across the waters. Do you believe that the Spirit of God still moves in this world and in our lives? What signs do you see of God's Spirit living and moving in your life? Living in the Spirit is an important part of the Christian journey. We travel not only with others, the faith community, but we also travel with God whose Spirit guides us on our way. May you experience the joy and growing awareness of the Spirit of God in your life as you continue the baptismal journey of faith and life.

2. Journal Notes

Use a pen or pencil to write a response for each of the following:

1. A time in my life when I believe that God helped me was . . .

2. In the future, with God's help, I know that I can . . .

3. Jesus compared the Holy Spirit to a "wind [blowing] where it chooses" (John 3:8). Some ways I think the Spirit of God is like the wind include . . .

4. Jesus also described the Spirit as a helper (John 14:16). A time in the future when I know I will need God's Spirit to help me is . . .

5. Jesus also taught that the Holy Spirit is a guide and companion on the journey of life (John 14:26). Right now I need God's guidance to help me . . .

6. Some questions I have about the Holy Spirit are . . .

7. This is what I believe about the Spirit of God . . .

8. A person I know whose life reflects the Spirit of God is _____.
Explain how:

3. Talk and Listen

When you both have finished writing, take turns talking about each of your responses.

4. Scripture Talk

By this we know that we abide in him and he in us, because he has given us of his Spirit.
1 John 4:13

Discuss

1. If someone asked me to describe the Spirit of God, I would say that the Spirit of God is like . . .

2. To say that I have the Spirit of Christ abiding or living in me means that . . .

3. Signs of this in anyone's life include . . .

5. Continue on Side 2

If you have time, continue with Side 2. If not, come back to Side 2 in the near future.

Living in the Spirit

1. What Is This?

The Third Article says, "I believe in the Holy Spirit . . ." Luther asks, "What is this?" And then writes: "I believe that by my own understanding or strength I cannot believe in Jesus Christ my Lord or come to him, but instead the Holy Spirit has called me through the gospel, enlightened me with his gifts, made me holy, and kept me in the true faith."

Discuss

1. God's Spirit calls me through the gospel, that is, the good news that I am forgiven and loved by God. To be forgiven and loved by God means . . .

2. We are not holy, but the Holy Spirit makes us holy. To be "holy" means . . .

3. The Holy Spirit also reveals "true faith" to me. In other words, I am able to believe in the truth of the Christian faith because . . .

2. Journal Notes

Use a pen or pencil to write a response for each of the following:

In Galatians 5:22 (look up and read), Paul lists some of the "fruit" or qualities present in our lives when God's Spirit is active and living in us. For each quality below, try to write a simple definition, followed by an example of the evidence of this fruit in your own life.

1. Love is . . .

Example from my life:

2. Joy is . . .

Example from my life:

3. Peace is . . .

Example:

4. Patience is . . .

Example:

5. Kindness is . . .

Example:

6. Generosity is . . .

Example:

7. Faithfulness is . . .

Example:

8. Gentleness is . . .

Example:

9. Self-control is . . .

Example:

3. Talk and Listen

When you both have finished writing, take turns talking about each of your responses.

4. If You Have Time, Talk About . . .

1. If I had an orchard, I would keep the trees in my orchard healthy and fruitful by . . .

2. My life has been fruitful and productive in the following ways:

3. These things might help my life to become more healthy and fruitful:

Living in the Spirit

1. Introduction

Genesis 1:2 describes the Spirit of the Creator God as moving across the waters. Do you believe that the Spirit of God still moves in this world and in our lives? What signs do you see of God's Spirit living and moving in your life? Living in the Spirit is an important part of the Christian journey. We travel not only with others, the faith community, but we also travel with God whose Spirit guides us on our way. May you experience the joy and growing awareness of the Spirit of God in your life as you continue the baptismal journey of faith and life.

2. Journal Notes

Use a pen or pencil to write a response for each of the following:

1. A time in my life when I believe that God helped me was . . .

2. In the future, with God's help, I know that I can . . .

3. Jesus compared the Holy Spirit to a "wind [blowing] where it chooses" (John 3:8). Some ways I think the Spirit of God is like the wind include . . .

4. Jesus also described the Spirit as a helper (John 14:16). A time in the future when I know I will need God's Spirit to help me is . . .

5. Jesus also taught that the Holy Spirit is a guide and companion on the journey of life (John 14:26). Right now I need God's guidance to help me . . .

6. Some questions I have about the Holy Spirit are . . .

7. This is what I believe about the Spirit of God . . .

8. A person I know whose life reflects the Spirit of God is _____.
Explain how:

3. Talk and Listen

When you both have finished writing, take turns talking about each of your responses.

4. Scripture Talk

By this we know that we abide in him and he in us, because he has given us of his Spirit.
1 John 4:13

Discuss

1. If someone asked me to describe the Spirit of God, I would say that the Spirit of God is like . . .

2. To say that I have the Spirit of Christ abiding or living in me means that . . .

3. Signs of this in anyone's life include . . .

5. Continue on Side 2

If you have time, continue with Side 2. If not, come back to Side 2 in the near future.

Living in the Spirit

1. What Is This?

The Third Article says, "I believe in the Holy Spirit . . ." Luther asks, "What is this?" And then writes: "I believe that by my own understanding or strength I cannot believe in Jesus Christ my Lord or come to him, but instead the Holy Spirit has called me through the gospel, enlightened me with his gifts, made me holy, and kept me in the true faith."

Discuss

1. God's Spirit calls me through the gospel, that is, the good news that I am forgiven and loved by God. To be forgiven and loved by God means . . .

2. We are not holy, but the Holy Spirit makes us holy. To be "holy" means . . .

3. The Holy Spirit also reveals "true faith" to me. In other words, I am able to believe in the truth of the Christian faith because . . .

2. Journal Notes

Use a pen or pencil to write a response for each of the following:

In Galatians 5:22 (look up and read), Paul lists some of the "fruit" or qualities present in our lives when God's Spirit is active and living in us. For each quality below, try to write a simple definition, followed by an example of the evidence of this fruit in your own life.

1. Love is . . .

Example from my life:

2. Joy is . . .

Example from my life:

3. Peace is . . .

Example:

4. Patience is . . .

Example:

5. Kindness is . . .

Example:

6. Generosity is . . .

Example:

7. Faithfulness is . . .

Example:

8. Gentleness is . . .

Example:

9. Self-control is . . .

Example:

3. Talk and Listen

When you both have finished writing, take turns talking about each of your responses.

4. If You Have Time, Talk About . . .

1. If I had an orchard, I would keep the trees in my orchard healthy and fruitful by . . .

2. My life has been fruitful and productive in the following ways:

3. These things might help my life to become more healthy and fruitful:

My Beliefs

1. Introduction

Our beliefs are like directional signs that guide us down the road of life. They remind us of who we are, what's important to us, and where we want to go with our lives. To be confirmed in the faith is to recognize that our Christian beliefs are among the most important road signs that guide our lives.

We're old enough now to believe for ourselves the faith that was washed over us at our baptism. May God continue to confirm within you the beliefs that, like directional signs, guide your life to deeper faith, hope, and love.

2. Journal Notes

Use a pen or pencil to write a response for each of the following:

For me, to "believe" something means that I . . .

Try to write a personal belief statement for each of the following:

1. Creation of the world: I believe . . .

2. God: I believe . . .

3. Jesus Christ: I believe . . .

4. The Holy Spirit: I believe . . .

5. Sin and evil: I believe . . .

6. Forgiveness: I believe . . .

7. Prayer: I believe . . .

8. Baptism: I believe . . .

9. The Bible: I believe . . .

10. Death: I believe . . .

11. Suffering: I believe . . .

12. I find it hard to believe that . . .

3. Talk and Listen

When you both have finished writing, take turns talking about each of your responses.

4. Scripture Talk

And now faith, hope, and love abide, these three; and the greatest of these is love.
1 Corinthians 13:13

Discuss

1. My own definition of *faith* is . . .

2. I would define *hope* as . . .

3. Here's how I would describe *love:*

5. Continue on Side 2

If you have time, continue with Side 2. If not, come back to Side 2 in the near future.

My Beliefs

1. What Is This?

The Second Article of the Apostles' Creed reads: "I believe in Jesus Christ, his only Son, our Lord. He was conceived by the power of the Holy Spirit and born of the virgin Mary. He suffered under Pontius Pilate, was crucified, died, and was buried. He descended into hell. On the third day he rose again . . ." To this Luther adds: "I believe that Jesus Christ, true God, begotten of the Father in eternity, and also true human being, born of the virgin Mary, is my Lord. He has redeemed me . . ."

1. Discuss the difference between knowing something scientifically, and knowing something by believing it.

2. What are some of the things we can't see, and yet we believe in them?

3. How do we come to believe something?

2. Journal Notes

Use a pen or pencil to write a response for each of the following:

Additional Personal Beliefs

1. I believe that being active in my faith community helps me to . . .

2. I believe that receiving Holy Communion helps me to . . .

3. I believe that sharing my talents and financial resources in the work of God is important because . . .

4. I believe that it's important to be confirmed because it shows that . . .

5. I believe that God has given me the ability to . . .

6. I believe that in the future God wants me to . . .

7. I believe that doubts and questions about faith help us to . . .

8. I believe that for me to grow in my faith, I need to . . .

9. I believe that God wants to help me . . .

10. This is my prayer for the future: Dear God, help me to . . .

3. Talk and Listen

When you both have finished writing, take turns talking about each of your responses.

4. Scripture Talk

Discuss John 3:16: **[Jesus said], "For God so loved the world that he gave his only Son, so that everyone who believes in him may not perish but may have eternal life."**

5. If You Have Time, Talk About . . .

1. I believe that for me to be successful in life, I need to . . .

2. I believe that when I'm old, I'll be able to look back on my life and say . . .

3. I believe that one of the biggest problems facing the church today is . . .

4. I believe that one of the biggest problems facing the world today is . . .

My Beliefs

1. Introduction

Our beliefs are like directional signs that guide us down the road of life. They remind us of who we are, what's important to us, and where we want to go with our lives. To be confirmed in the faith is to recognize that our Christian beliefs are among the most important road signs that guide our lives.

We're old enough now to believe for ourselves the faith that was washed over us at our baptism. May God continue to confirm within you the beliefs that, like directional signs, guide your life to deeper faith, hope, and love.

2. Journal Notes

Use a pen or pencil to write a response for each of the following:

For me, to "believe" something means that I . . .

Try to write a personal belief statement for each of the following:

1. Creation of the world: I believe . . .

2. God: I believe . . .

3. Jesus Christ: I believe . . .

4. The Holy Spirit: I believe . . .

5. Sin and evil: I believe . . .

6. Forgiveness: I believe . . .

7. Prayer: I believe . . .

8. Baptism: I believe . . .

9. The Bible: I believe . . .

10. Death: I believe . . .

11. Suffering: I believe . . .

12. I find it hard to believe that . . .

3. Talk and Listen

When you both have finished writing, take turns talking about each of your responses.

4. Scripture Talk

And now faith, hope, and love abide, these three; and the greatest of these is love.
1 Corinthians 13:13

Discuss

1. My own definition of *faith* is . . .

2. I would define *hope* as . . .

3. Here's how I would describe *love:*

5. Continue on Side 2

If you have time, continue with Side 2. If not, come back to Side 2 in the near future.

My Beliefs

1. What Is This?

The Second Article of the Apostles' Creed reads: "I believe in Jesus Christ, his only Son, our Lord. He was conceived by the power of the Holy Spirit and born of the virgin Mary. He suffered under Pontius Pilate, was crucified, died, and was buried. He descended into hell. On the third day he rose again . . ." To this Luther adds: "I believe that Jesus Christ, true God, begotten of the Father in eternity, and also true human being, born of the virgin Mary, is my Lord. He has redeemed me . . ."

1. Discuss the difference between knowing something scientifically, and knowing something by believing it.

2. What are some of the things we can't see, and yet we believe in them?

3. How do we come to believe something?

2. Journal Notes

Use a pen or pencil to write a response for each of the following:

Additional Personal Beliefs

1. I believe that being active in my faith community helps me to . . .

2. I believe that receiving Holy Communion helps me to . . .

3. I believe that sharing my talents and financial resources in the work of God is important because . . .

4. I believe that it's important to be confirmed because it shows that . . .

5. I believe that God has given me the ability to . . .

6. I believe that in the future God wants me to . . .

7. I believe that doubts and questions about faith help us to . . .

8. I believe that for me to grow in my faith, I need to . . .

9. I believe that God wants to help me . . .

10. This is my prayer for the future: Dear God, help me to . . .

3. Talk and Listen

When you both have finished writing, take turns talking about each of your responses.

4. Scripture Talk

Discuss John 3:16: **[Jesus said], "For God so loved the world that he gave his only Son, so that everyone who believes in him may not perish but may have eternal life."**

5. If You Have Time, Talk About . . .

1. I believe that for me to be successful in life, I need to . . .

2. I believe that when I'm old, I'll be able to look back on my life and say . . .

3. I believe that one of the biggest problems facing the church today is . . .

4. I believe that one of the biggest problems facing the world today is . . .

Saying Yes

1. Introduction

Yes is one of the most powerful words in any language. You can spend a lifetime thinking about going somewhere; but until you say yes to the journey and start traveling, you will find it hard to reach your destination. The Christian life is all about saying yes to the journey begun in Baptism and yes to traveling the way of Jesus Christ. When we do, we experience wonderful sights and sounds along the way that we might have missed if we had said no. May God be with you as you continue to say yes to your baptismal faith and yes to following Jesus.

2. Journal Notes

Use a pen or pencil to write a response for each of the following:

1. Saying yes to being a good student or a good employee is a commitment or promise to . . .

2. Saying yes to my baptismal journey is a promise or commitment to . . .

3. Saying yes to following Jesus as the leader of my life is a promise to . . .

4. Saying yes to confirmation has helped me to . . .

Think carefully about some of the promises you are willing to make, and then express them below:

5. I promise Jesus Christ that I will . . .

6. I promise my faith community that I will . . .

7. I promise to serve and help others by . . .

8. In addition, I promise that I will always try to . . .

3. Talk and Listen

When you both have finished writing, take turns talking about each of your responses.

4. Scripture Talk

Discuss Matthew 4:19-20: **And [Jesus] said to them, "Follow me, and I will make you fish for people." Immediately they left their nets and followed him.**

Discuss

1. I think "fish for people" means . . .

2. Some of the "nets" (or attitudes and priorities) I might need to leave behind in order to follow Jesus include . . .

5. Continue on Side 2

If you have time, continue with Side 2. If not, come back to Side 2 in the near future.

Saying Yes

1. What Is This?

The conclusion of the Lord's Prayer goes, "For the kingdom, the power, and the glory are yours, now and forever. Amen"

"What is this?" Martin Luther asks, and goes on to answer: "That I should be certain that such petitions are acceptable to and heard by our Father in heaven, for God himself commanded us to pray like this and has promised to hear us. 'Amen, amen' means 'Yes, yes, it is going to come about just like this.'"

Discuss what you believe it means to say amen or yes to living for the kingdom, the power, and the glory of God.

2. Journal Notes

Use a pen or pencil to write a response for each of the following:

For each of the following spiritual disciplines (activities that are a way of saying yes to growing in the Christian faith), list a goal for improvement or growth:

Spiritual Discipline   My Goal

Attending worship

Daily devotional and prayer time

Studying the Bible

Giving money for God's work

Loving others

Serving my family

Serving others

Witnessing and inviting others to church

This is my prayer for spiritual growth:
Dear God, . . .

3. Talk and Listen

When you both have finished writing, take turns talking about each of your responses.

4. Scripture Talk

Discuss Philippians 3:14-16: **I press on toward the goal for the prize of the heavenly call of God in Christ Jesus. Let those of us then who are mature be of the same mind . . . let us hold fast to what we have attained.**

1. I would say that the main goal of a Christian is to . . .

2. To be mature in my Christian faith means that I . . .

3. I think I'm supposed to "hold fast" to (what?) and let go of (what?) . . .

Saying Yes

1. Introduction

Yes is one of the most powerful words in any language. You can spend a lifetime thinking about going somewhere; but until you say yes to the journey and start traveling, you will find it hard to reach your destination. The Christian life is all about saying yes to the journey begun in Baptism and yes to traveling the way of Jesus Christ. When we do, we experience wonderful sights and sounds along the way that we might have missed if we had said no. May God be with you as you continue to say yes to your baptismal faith and yes to following Jesus.

2. Journal Notes

Use a pen or pencil to write a response for each of the following:

1. Saying yes to being a good student or a good employee is a commitment or promise to . . .

2. Saying yes to my baptismal journey is a promise or commitment to . . .

3. Saying yes to following Jesus as the leader of my life is a promise to . . .

4. Saying yes to confirmation has helped me to . . .

Think carefully about some of the promises you are willing to make, and then express them below:

5. I promise Jesus Christ that I will . . .

6. I promise my faith community that I will . . .

7. I promise to serve and help others by . . .

8. In addition, I promise that I will always try to . . .

3. Talk and Listen

When you both have finished writing, take turns talking about each of your responses.

4. Scripture Talk

Discuss Matthew 4:19-20: **And [Jesus] said to them, "Follow me, and I will make you fish for people." Immediately they left their nets and followed him.**

Discuss

1. I think "fish for people" means . . .

2. Some of the "nets" (or attitudes and priorities) I might need to leave behind in order to follow Jesus include . . .

5. Continue on Side 2

If you have time, continue with Side 2. If not, come back to Side 2 in the near future.

Saying Yes

1. What Is This?

The conclusion of the Lord's Prayer goes, "For the kingdom, the power, and the glory are yours, now and forever. Amen"

"What is this?" Martin Luther asks, and goes on to answer: "That I should be certain that such petitions are acceptable to and heard by our Father in heaven, for God himself commanded us to pray like this and has promised to hear us. 'Amen, amen' means 'Yes, yes, it is going to come about just like this.' "

Discuss what you believe it means to say amen or yes to living for the kingdom, the power, and the glory of God.

2. Journal Notes

Use a pen or pencil to write a response for each of the following:

For each of the following spiritual disciplines (activities that are a way of saying yes to growing in the Christian faith), list a goal for improvement or growth:

Spiritual Discipline   My Goal

Attending
worship

Daily
devotional
and prayer
time

Studying
the Bible

Giving money
for God's work

Loving
others

Serving
my family

Serving
others

Witnessing and
inviting others
to church

This is my prayer for spiritual growth:
Dear God, . . .

3. Talk and Listen

When you both have finished writing, take turns talking about each of your responses.

4. Scripture Talk

Discuss Philippians 3:14-16: **I press on toward the goal for the prize of the heavenly call of God in Christ Jesus. Let those of us then who are mature be of the same mind . . . let us hold fast to what we have attained.**

1. I would say that the main goal of a Christian is to . . .

2. To be mature in my Christian faith means that I . . .

3. I think I'm supposed to "hold fast" to (what?) and let go of (what?) . . .

Being a Lutheran

1. Introduction

"Where do you go to church?"

"Oh, I'm a Lutheran."

"Lutheran? What's that?"

Behind the answer to that question is a long history of faith and tradition. Do you know what is unique and special about those who have journeyed the Christian way with the name Lutheran? What do Lutherans stand for and believe? In this conversation you will have a chance to talk about being justified by grace through faith, the central theme of Lutheran belief. You will discuss some of the important teachings of Martin Luther, the principal figure in the Protestant Reformation during the 16th century.

2. Journal Notes

Use a pen or pencil to write a response for each of the following:

1. I started attending a Lutheran congregation (how long ago?) . . .

Some reasons I/we choose to continue to attend a Lutheran congregation include . . .

2. One of the traditions of my faith community that I really like is . . .

3. If someone asked me, "Why are you Lutheran?" I might tell him or her that . . .

4. One person who accepts me pretty much the way I am is _____.
I feel accepted or welcomed by this person because she or he . . .

5. A time when I was loved and accepted by someone, even when I knew I didn't deserve it, was . . .

6. Just believing that God accepts, loves, and forgives me, even when I don't deserve it, can help me to . . .

7. My definition for the word *grace* is (look up in a dictionary, if necessary) . . .

8. My definition for the word *justified* is (look up, if necessary) . . .

9. To say that I am justified by grace through faith means that God . . .

10. Lutherans believe that our salvation is nothing more than a gift of God's grace. For me to say, "I'm saved by grace," means that I . . .

3. Talk and Listen

When you both have finished writing, take turns talking about each of your responses.

4. Scripture Talk

Discuss Ephesians 2:8 and tell each other what you think it means: **For by grace you have been saved through faith, and this is not your own doing; it is the gift of God.**

5. Continue on Side 2

If you have time, continue with Side 2. If not, come back to Side 2 in the near future.

Being a Lutheran

1. What Is This?

Maybe you have heard this quote from Martin Luther's writings: "A Christian is a perfectly free lord of all, subject to none. A Christian is a perfectly dutiful servant of all, subject to all."*

What is this? Luther draws from Paul's writings in 1 Corinthians 9:19: "For though I am free with respect to all, I have made myself a slave to all, so that I might win more of them." And Romans 13:8: "Owe no one anything, except to love one another; for the one who loves another has fulfilled the law." Luther says, "Love by its very nature is ready to serve and be subject to [the one] who is loved. So Christ, although he was Lord of all . . . was at the same time a free man and a servant."*

*From "The Freedom of a Christian," in *Martin Luther's Basic Theological Writings,* ed. Timothy F. Lull (Minneapolis: Fortress Press, 1989), 596.

2. Journal Notes

Use a pen or pencil to write a response for each of the following:

Perfectly Free

1. I feel really free when I'm . . .

2. But I don't feel very free when . . .

3. Article IV of the Augsburg Confession says that Lutherans "teach that human beings cannot be justified [made right] before God by their own powers, merits, or works. But they are justified as a gift on account of Christ through faith when they believe that . . . their sins are forgiven on account of Christ, who by his death made satisfaction for our sins." (From the Augsburg Confession, Article IV [Latin Text], in *The Book of Concord* [Minneapolis: Fortress Press, 2000], 39 and 41.) Sin has a way of destroying our freedom, but when I am forgiven by God or someone I have wronged, I am able to feel free again. Why?

An example from my own life was the time . . .

4. In John 8:36, Jesus says, "So if the Son makes you free, you will be free indeed." According to Jesus, in order for me to be "perfectly free," I need . . .

Perfectly Servant

5. Jesus lived his life as a servant to others. Some of the ways he served and helped others include . . .

6. One way we show love for others is by serving them. Some of the people who show their love for me by serving and helping me include . . .

Examples of how I am served are . . .

7. I show love for God and others by serving or helping (who? how?) . . .

8. Serving others takes the focus off of me and directs it toward others. The result of this is often a freedom from self. This is my "servant's prayer": Dear God, . . .

3. Talk and Listen

When you both have finished writing, take turns talking about each of your responses.

4. Scripture Talk

Discuss Romans 3:22-24: **For there is no distinction, since all have sinned and fall short of the glory of God; they are now justified by his grace as a gift, through the redemption that is in Christ Jesus.**

1. I would describe sin as . . .

2. Examples of sin from my own life include . . .

3. To be justified is to be accepted and loved just as I am by God, even though I don't deserve it. Knowing that God accepts and loves me gives me the freedom to . . .

Being a Lutheran

1. Introduction

"Where do you go to church?"

"Oh, I'm a Lutheran."

"Lutheran? What's that?"

Behind the answer to that question is a long history of faith and tradition. Do you know what is unique and special about those who have journeyed the Christian way with the name Lutheran? What do Lutherans stand for and believe? In this conversation you will have a chance to talk about being justified by grace through faith, the central theme of Lutheran belief. You will discuss some of the important teachings of Martin Luther, the principal figure in the Protestant Reformation during the 16th century.

2. Journal Notes

Use a pen or pencil to write a response for each of the following:

1. I started attending a Lutheran congregation (how long ago?) . . .

Some reasons I/we choose to continue to attend a Lutheran congregation include . . .

2. One of the traditions of my faith community that I really like is . . .

3. If someone asked me, "Why are you Lutheran?" I might tell him or her that . . .

4. One person who accepts me pretty much the way I am is _____.
I feel accepted or welcomed by this person because she or he . . .

5. A time when I was loved and accepted by someone, even when I knew I didn't deserve it, was . . .

6. Just believing that God accepts, loves, and forgives me, even when I don't deserve it, can help me to . . .

7. My definition for the word *grace* is (look up in a dictionary, if necessary) . . .

8. My definition for the word *justified* is (look up, if necessary) . . .

9. To say that I am justified by grace through faith means that God . . .

10. Lutherans believe that our salvation is nothing more than a gift of God's grace. For me to say, "I'm saved by grace," means that I . . .

3. Talk and Listen

When you both have finished writing, take turns talking about each of your responses.

4. Scripture Talk

Discuss Ephesians 2:8 and tell each other what you think it means: **For by grace you have been saved through faith, and this is not your own doing; it is the gift of God.**

5. Continue on Side 2

If you have time, continue with Side 2. If not, come back to Side 2 in the near future.

Being a Lutheran

1. What Is This?

Maybe you have heard this quote from Martin Luther's writings: "A Christian is a perfectly free lord of all, subject to none. A Christian is a perfectly dutiful servant of all, subject to all."*

What is this? Luther draws from Paul's writings in 1 Corinthians 9:19: "For though I am free with respect to all, I have made myself a slave to all, so that I might win more of them." And Romans 13:8: "Owe no one anything, except to love one another; for the one who loves another has fulfilled the law." Luther says, "Love by its very nature is ready to serve and be subject to [the one] who is loved. So Christ, although he was Lord of all . . . was at the same time a free man and a servant."*

*From "The Freedom of a Christian," in *Martin Luther's Basic Theological Writings,* ed. Timothy F. Lull (Minneapolis: Fortress Press, 1989), 596.

2. Journal Notes

Use a pen or pencil to write a response for each of the following:

Perfectly Free

1. I feel really free when I'm . . .

2. But I don't feel very free when . . .

3. Article IV of the Augsburg Confession says that Lutherans "teach that human beings cannot be justified [made right] before God by their own powers, merits, or works. But they are justified as a gift on account of Christ through faith when they believe that . . . their sins are forgiven on account of Christ, who by his death made satisfaction for our sins." (From the Augsburg Confession, Article IV [Latin Text], in *The Book of Concord* [Minneapolis: Fortress Press, 2000], 39 and 41.) Sin has a way of destroying our freedom, but when I am forgiven by God or someone I have wronged, I am able to feel free again. Why?

An example from my own life was the time . . .

4. In John 8:36, Jesus says, "So if the Son makes you free, you will be free indeed." According to Jesus, in order for me to be "perfectly free," I need . . .

Perfectly Servant

5. Jesus lived his life as a servant to others. Some of the ways he served and helped others include . . .

6. One way we show love for others is by serving them. Some of the people who show their love for me by serving and helping me include . . .

Examples of how I am served are . . .

7. I show love for God and others by serving or helping (who? how?) . . .

8. Serving others takes the focus off of me and directs it toward others. The result of this is often a freedom from self. This is my "servant's prayer": Dear God, . . .

3. Talk and Listen

When you both have finished writing, take turns talking about each of your responses.

4. Scripture Talk

Discuss Romans 3:22-24: **For there is no distinction, since all have sinned and fall short of the glory of God; they are now justified by his grace as a gift, through the redemption that is in Christ Jesus.**

1. I would describe sin as . . .

2. Examples of sin from my own life include . . .

3. To be justified is to be accepted and loved just as I am by God, even though I don't deserve it. Knowing that God accepts and loves me gives me the freedom to . . .

Staying in Touch with God

1. Introduction

What do you do to stay spiritually motivated, and what helps you stay in touch with God? Like the gasoline in the tank that keeps a motor running, staying in touch with God gives us fuel for the baptismal journey of life and faith. We need to be open and receptive to God and filled with the good things of God that give energy to our soul as we journey Christ's way. May you know the energy and goodness that come from keeping your relationship with God growing and alive.

2. Journal Notes

Use a pen or pencil to write a response for each of the following:

1. Someone I like to "stay in touch with" is
_____. Some things that
help people to "stay in touch" include . . .

2. Some of the things that help me stay in touch with God include . . .

Friends help us stay in touch with God!
3. Friends know us, accept us, and help us. A person I consider to be a good Christian friend is _____. We both benefit from our friendship in the following ways:

4. Christian friends can help each other stay in touch with God by . . .

5. I think my friendship with you has helped me to . . .

Prayer helps us stay in touch with God.
6. Friendship with God is a lot like other friendships. Spending time with God helps keep our friendship going. Prayer is a way to spend time with God. If someone asked me to describe my prayer life, I would say . . .

7. I could improve my ability to pray if I would take the time to . . .

After you have talked about the above items, take time to pray in silence following this step-by-step plan:

1. First, think about God's awesome love and greatness.

2. Express things you are thankful for.

3. Ask God to forgive you for things you have done or failed to do.

4. Ask God to help you and others you know who need God's help and guidance.

3. Talk and Listen

When you both have finished writing, take turns talking about each of your responses.

4. Scripture Talk

Let the word of Christ dwell in you richly; teach and admonish one another in all wisdom; and with gratitude in your hearts sing psalms, hymns, and spiritual songs to God. Colossians 3:16

Discuss

1. To "let the word of Christ dwell" in me means that I need to . . .

2. Someone I know who helps me understand the word of Christ is . . .

3. I'm grateful to God for . . .

5. Continue on Side 2

If you have time, continue with Side 2. If not, come back to Side 2 in the near future.

Staying in Touch with God

1. What Is This?

Martin Luther believed that each person in the household needed to have regular daily devotions, so he suggested in his Small Catechism a daily prayer form for morning and evening:

1. In the morning, as soon as you get out of bed, you are to make the sign of the cross, and say: "Under the care of God the Father, Son, and Holy Spirit. Amen." Then say the Apostles' Creed, the Lord's Prayer, a morning prayer, and a hymn.

Luther writes that after this devotion, "you are to go to your work joyfully."

2. In the evening when you go to bed, make the sign of the cross, say the invocation, the Apostles' Creed, the Lord's Prayer, and an evening prayer. "Then you are to go to sleep quickly and cheerfully."

Discuss with each other your own daily pattern of devotion, or talk about some of the ways you might grow in this area of spiritual discipline.

2. Journal Notes

Use a pen or pencil to write a response for each of the following:

The Bible helps us stay in touch with God.

1. To me, saying that the Bible is God's Word means that . . .

2. The Bible can help me stay in touch with God if I take the time to . . .

3. I would enjoy reading the Bible more if . . .

4. One of the most interesting ways I've found to read and study the Bible is . . .

5. Some questions I have about the Bible are . . .

Worship helps us stay in touch with God.

6. If someone asked me to define the word *worship*, I would say worship is . . .

7. I know that I'm worshiping God when I . . .

8. Participating regularly in the worship of the faith community can help me stay in touch with God by . . .

9. I have felt especially close to God when . . .

10. The best time of the day for me to devote to daily worship (Bible reading and prayer) is . . .

11. My prayer is: Help me to improve my relationship with you, dear God, by . . .

3. Talk and Listen

When you both have finished writing, take turns talking about each of your responses.

4. Scripture Talk

Discuss John 8:31: **[Jesus said], "If you continue in my word, you are truly my disciples; and you will know the truth, and the truth will make you free."**

5. If You Have Time, Talk About . . .

1. My favorite part of the Bible is . . .

2. When I read the Bible, it's sometimes hard for me to . . .

3. For me the most interesting part of our worship service is when . . .

4. I think our worship services might be more meaningful and interesting to me if . . .

Staying in Touch with God

1. Introduction

What do you do to stay spiritually motivated, and what helps you stay in touch with God? Like the gasoline in the tank that keeps a motor running, staying in touch with God gives us fuel for the baptismal journey of life and faith. We need to be open and receptive to God and filled with the good things of God that give energy to our soul as we journey Christ's way. May you know the energy and goodness that come from keeping your relationship with God growing and alive.

2. Journal Notes

Use a pen or pencil to write a response for each of the following:

1. Someone I like to "stay in touch with" is _____. Some things that help people to "stay in touch" include . . .

2. Some of the things that help me stay in touch with God include . . .

Friends help us stay in touch with God!
3. Friends know us, accept us, and help us. A person I consider to be a good Christian friend is _____. We both benefit from our friendship in the following ways:

4. Christian friends can help each other stay in touch with God by . . .

5. I think my friendship with you has helped me to . . .

Prayer helps us stay in touch with God.
6. Friendship with God is a lot like other friendships. Spending time with God helps keep our friendship going. Prayer is a way to spend time with God. If someone asked me to describe my prayer life, I would say . . .

7. I could improve my ability to pray if I would take the time to . . .

After you have talked about the above items, take time to pray in silence following this step-by-step plan:

1. First, think about God's awesome love and greatness.

2. Express things you are thankful for.

3. Ask God to forgive you for things you have done or failed to do.

4. Ask God to help you and others you know who need God's help and guidance.

3. Talk and Listen

When you both have finished writing, take turns talking about each of your responses.

4. Scripture Talk

Let the word of Christ dwell in you richly; teach and admonish one another in all wisdom; and with gratitude in your hearts sing psalms, hymns, and spiritual songs to God. Colossians 3:16

Discuss

1. To "let the word of Christ dwell" in me means that I need to . . .

2. Someone I know who helps me understand the word of Christ is . . .

3. I'm grateful to God for . . .

5. Continue on Side 2

If you have time, continue with Side 2. If not, come back to Side 2 in the near future.

Staying in Touch with God

1. What Is This?

Martin Luther believed that each person in the household needed to have regular daily devotions, so he suggested in his Small Catechism a daily prayer form for morning and evening:

1. In the morning, as soon as you get out of bed, you are to make the sign of the cross, and say: "Under the care of God the Father, Son, and Holy Spirit. Amen." Then say the Apostles' Creed, the Lord's Prayer, a morning prayer, and a hymn.

Luther writes that after this devotion, "you are to go to your work joyfully."

2. In the evening when you go to bed, make the sign of the cross, say the invocation, the Apostles' Creed, the Lord's Prayer, and an evening prayer. "Then you are to go to sleep quickly and cheerfully."

Discuss with each other your own daily pattern of devotion, or talk about some of the ways you might grow in this area of spiritual discipline.

2. Journal Notes

Use a pen or pencil to write a response for each of the following:

The Bible helps us stay in touch with God.

1. To me, saying that the Bible is God's Word means that . . .

2. The Bible can help me stay in touch with God if I take the time to . . .

3. I would enjoy reading the Bible more if . . .

4. One of the most interesting ways I've found to read and study the Bible is . . .

5. Some questions I have about the Bible are . . .

Worship helps us stay in touch with God.

6. If someone asked me to define the word *worship,* I would say worship is . . .

7. I know that I'm worshiping God when I . . .

8. Participating regularly in the worship of the faith community can help me stay in touch with God by . . .

9. I have felt especially close to God when . . .

10. The best time of the day for me to devote to daily worship (Bible reading and prayer) is . . .

11. My prayer is: Help me to improve my relationship with you, dear God, by . . .

3. Talk and Listen

When you both have finished writing, take turns talking about each of your responses.

4. Scripture Talk

Discuss John 8:31: **[Jesus said], "If you continue in my word, you are truly my disciples; and you will know the truth, and the truth will make you free."**

5. If You Have Time, Talk About . . .

1. My favorite part of the Bible is . . .

2. When I read the Bible, it's sometimes hard for me to . . .

3. For me the most interesting part of our worship service is when . . .

4. I think our worship services might be more meaningful and interesting to me if . . .

Life Beyond Confirmation

1. Introduction

The Christian journey is a lifelong process, with new horizons always inviting you to continue. In the Christian journey there will always be new experiences, challenges, and insights waiting for you around each bend in the road. As you join heart and hand in friendship with others who travel the Christian way of love, service, and life, may you always grow in your awareness of God's guiding Spirit. Enjoy the trip!

2. Journal Notes

Use a pen or pencil to write a response for each of the following:

1. Looking back on our journey together as we have discussed life and faith, I have especially enjoyed . . .

2. I think one of the most important things I have learned or discovered in our discussions is . . .

3. One of the important commitments or promises I have made is to . . .

4. During the next year I want to grow in my Christian life by . . .

5. And I want to be more involved in my faith community by . . .

6. Some of the talents and qualities I have learned to appreciate about you (gifts that God can use in service to others to make this a better world) include . . .

7. Some of the talents, interests, and qualities I see in myself that God can use include . . .

8. I believe that God will help me as I journey through life in the following ways:

3. Talk and Listen

When you both have finished writing, take turns talking about each of your responses.

4. Scripture Talk

Discuss Philippians 3:13-14: **Beloved, I do not consider that I have made it my own; but this one thing I do: forgetting what lies behind and straining forward to what lies ahead, I press on toward the goal for the prize of the heavenly call of God in Christ Jesus.**

1. As I look at my past, some of the experiences of life and faith that are behind me include . . .

2. As I look toward the future, experiences of life and faith that lie ahead of me include . . .

5. Continue on Side 2

If you have time, continue with Side 2. If not, come back to Side 2 in the near future.

Life Beyond Confirmation

1. What Is This?

Martin Luther quotes the first of the Ten Commandments, "You shall have no other gods," and then asks, "What is this? We are to fear [respect], love, and trust God above all things."

Discuss

1. Some of the things that get in the way of giving God top priority in my life include . . .

2. To me, to fear or respect God means . . .

3. To me, to love God means . . .

4. To me, to trust God means . . .

5. To me, "above all things" means . . .

2. Journal Notes

Use a pen or pencil to write a response for each of the following:

In Mark 9:35 Jesus teaches his disciples: "Whoever wants to be first must be last of all and servant of all."

1. I think Jesus must have needed to say that to his disciples because they . . .

2. Jesus calls us to serve others with our lives. When I serve others, I feel . . .

3. Lately, I have spent time serving in these ways (serving whom and how?):

4. I can serve others within the faith community by . . .

5. One of my dreams for the future is that I will be able to . . .

6. Right now my job or "vocation" (the thing that I spend most of my time doing) is . . .

I believe I am serving God in this vocation in the following ways:

7. The job, or calling, of every follower of Jesus is to . . .

8. As a part of my commitment to make Jesus Christ the most important person in my life and be influenced by his love and teachings, in the future I am willing to . . .

9. My prayer for the future is: Dear God, . . .

3. Talk and Listen

When you both have finished writing, take turns talking about each of your responses.

4. If You Have Time, Talk About . . .

1. On a separate sheet of paper, take time to write a letter to the person with whom you have been meeting. In the letter be sure to thank the other person, affirm and express what you appreciate about him or her, and give the person a blessing, telling what you hope God will do in her or his life.

2. If and when you are nearing the end of the mentor/youth relationship, try to find a time to celebrate by sharing some kind of food together as well as the letters you have written.

Life Beyond Confirmation

1. Introduction

The Christian journey is a lifelong process, with new horizons always inviting you to continue. In the Christian journey there will always be new experiences, challenges, and insights waiting for you around each bend in the road. As you join heart and hand in friendship with others who travel the Christian way of love, service, and life, may you always grow in your awareness of God's guiding Spirit. Enjoy the trip!

2. Journal Notes

Use a pen or pencil to write a response for each of the following:

1. Looking back on our journey together as we have discussed life and faith, I have especially enjoyed . . .

2. I think one of the most important things I have learned or discovered in our discussions is . . .

3. One of the important commitments or promises I have made is to . . .

4. During the next year I want to grow in my Christian life by . . .

5. And I want to be more involved in my faith community by . . .

6. Some of the talents and qualities I have learned to appreciate about you (gifts that God can use in service to others to make this a better world) include . . .

7. Some of the talents, interests, and qualities I see in myself that God can use include . . .

8. I believe that God will help me as I journey through life in the following ways:

3. Talk and Listen

When you both have finished writing, take turns talking about each of your responses.

4. Scripture Talk

Discuss Philippians 3:13-14: **Beloved, I do not consider that I have made it my own; but this one thing I do: forgetting what lies behind and straining forward to what lies ahead, I press on toward the goal for the prize of the heavenly call of God in Christ Jesus.**

1. As I look at my past, some of the experiences of life and faith that are behind me include . . .

2. As I look toward the future, experiences of life and faith that lie ahead of me include . . .

5. Continue on Side 2

If you have time, continue with Side 2. If not, come back to Side 2 in the near future.

Life Beyond Confirmation

1. What Is This?

Martin Luther quotes the first of the Ten Commandments, "You shall have no other gods," and then asks, "What is this? We are to fear [respect], love, and trust God above all things."

Discuss

1. Some of the things that get in the way of giving God top priority in my life include . . .

2. To me, to fear or respect God means . . .

3. To me, to love God means . . .

4. To me, to trust God means . . .

5. To me, "above all things" means . . .

2. Journal Notes

Use a pen or pencil to write a response for each of the following:

In Mark 9:35 Jesus teaches his disciples: "Whoever wants to be first must be last of all and servant of all."

1. I think Jesus must have needed to say that to his disciples because they . . .

2. Jesus calls us to serve others with our lives. When I serve others, I feel . . .

3. Lately, I have spent time serving in these ways (serving whom and how?):

4. I can serve others within the faith community by . . .

5. One of my dreams for the future is that I will be able to . . .

6. Right now my job or "vocation" (the thing that I spend most of my time doing) is . . .

I believe I am serving God in this vocation in the following ways:

7. The job, or calling, of every follower of Jesus is to . . .

8. As a part of my commitment to make Jesus Christ the most important person in my life and be influenced by his love and teachings, in the future I am willing to . . .

9. My prayer for the future is: Dear God, . . .

3. Talk and Listen

When you both have finished writing, take turns talking about each of your responses.

4. If You Have Time, Talk About . . .

1. On a separate sheet of paper, take time to write a letter to the person with whom you have been meeting. In the letter be sure to thank the other person, affirm and express what you appreciate about him or her, and give the person a blessing, telling what you hope God will do in her or his life.

2. If and when you are nearing the end of the mentor/youth relationship, try to find a time to celebrate by sharing some kind of food together as well as the letters you have written.